NOTES TO SELF

A 90-DAY DEVOTIONAL AND

Prayer Journal

FOR WOMEN

Activ8Her

This journal belongs to:

_____

Notes to Self

Copyright ©2023 by: Christine Garrett & Kolleen Lucariello, Co-Executive Directors, Activ8Her®, Inc.

Cindy Shipley Blaske's note cards used with permission. All rights reserved.

Published by: Activ8Her, Inc.
ISBN: 979-8-9890205-0-8

Cover and interior design by Michelle Rayburn (www.MissionandMedia.com)

Graphics for cover composition and interior from Storyblocks.com. Used by permission.

Dedicated to Cindy Shipley Blaske.
We love and miss you.

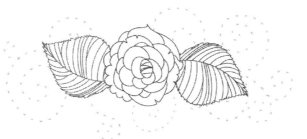

On your behalf Cindy, we dedicate
this journal to every single mom.

You are seen.
You are known.
You are loved.

Introduction

For over 25 years Cindy Shipley Blaske, Chrissy and I gathered around my kitchen table to dig into God's Word. I can't begin to count the Bible studies we've completed together which always led to conversations on theology and turned into a bit of therapy. We were hungry for transformation, each seeking to become the best version of our God-given identity. It would be rare for Cindy to miss writing a note to self on one of her blank note cards. If she didn't have a note card, she'd use her hand. Or arm.

Cindy was diagnosed with lung cancer in 2018 and our visits changed from sitting at my kitchen table to hospital visits and then eventually visits at her home. We'd talk through the happenings of our kids and what we'd heard in a teaching, but mostly, we just sat together, worshiped, and prayed. The day before she went home to Jesus, she made me promise I'd never let anyone say she "lost her battle with cancer," (she didn't. She fought incredibly hard but knew when it was time to meet her Savior). Her parting words to me were, "Kolleen, you and I are going to change the world." Cindy was one of our loudest cheerleaders for the ministry of Activ8Her, and one of the strongest, bravest single moms we know, this journal is the beginning of that change.

Cindy's Change. She had a heart for single moms because she was one. You don't need to be single to enjoy this journal, but if you are, the words from Cindy's note cards were hand written specifically to encourage you. May you be blessed by her insight and cared for by your Creator as you discover your identity in Christ.

— Kolleen

I met Cindy when she and her twins began attending the church my family attended. James and Allyssia were preschoolers and Cindy was already raising them on her own when we met.

One of Cindy's greatest desires from the moment we became friends was to have a husband with whom she could share her life with. While it was a desire all along, she had made the decision not to pursue that

goal until her children were grown. Determined, she stuck to it; although she would be the first to tell you that she did a fair share of whining about it. This became a topic of discussion at our Bible study table regularly. It was hard for her to remain faithful to the promise she'd made between her and the Lord. But she did it. Of the many attributes that I admired about Cindy, this would be the most admirable.

Even in those early Bible study days we prayed for the husband that God would bring when the time came. God was faithful to Cindy. The day came and she enjoyed the gift of marriage until she joined her Savior for eternity.

We have so many Cindy stories that we could probably write a whole book of those. They would be good stories and they would help you a lot. But, in this devotional, we believe we have laid out the principles Cindy would want you to know, in her own handwriting. You have in your hand years of wisdom she collected and wrote out; one 3x5 card after another. It is likely many of them were written as tears streamed down her face or she wrestled with frustration in her soul.

Our prayer for you as you make your way through these pages is that it will be a place where you can meet with God and wrestle with some things in your own soul for the glory of God. As you do, you will become part of Cindy's Change.

— *Chrissy*

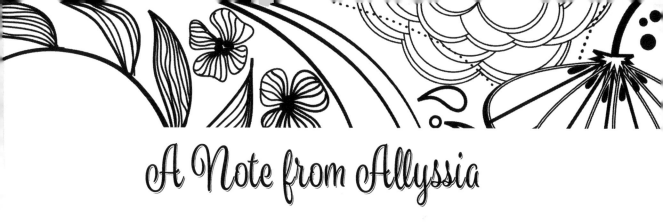

A Note from Allyssia

When I was asked to put together some thoughts about my mom I was humbled and honestly, I wasn't sure where to start. You see, my mom was my hero and my best friend. I learned so much through watching her example that it is hard to know where to begin. I hope I can adequately show you what made her the amazing and inspirational woman, friend, and mother she was.

My mom was single as she raised her twins. Somehow managing to do it all. She was an example of selflessness to everyone who knew her. I will always remember the sacrifices that she made for my brother and I, often going without so we could have what we needed, or perhaps fill a need for another mom. She always trusted in the Lord for our provision, and he was always faithful to honor her trust by providing for us!

Her faith in God was obvious and intentional. My mom had stacks and stacks of note cards on her desk; she even hung them on the bathroom mirror as reminders from the Lord. She'd carry a stack of 3x5 cards into church with her to jot down what she felt she'd heard from the Lord during service, or when a word from the pastor would encourage her later. I have fond memories of her taping the note cards on any visible surface around the entire house. One memory that sticks with me is seeing several note cards all with the word "THANKFUL" on them. This Impacted me greatly. She was always thankful to God even when we had very little. She filled her life with words from the Word, and in turn filled our world with them as well. It is not lost on me that her life wasn't falling apart because her Bible was.

She loved the Lord with all her heart. She would dance and sing so loud to Mandisa in the car I thought I would die of embarrassment. However, the older I became I began to join her in this craziness. Looking back now, I love that we shared those moments.

My mom loved others deeply. She had a heart to help provide for other single moms. To this day I still don't know how she did what she did while raising my brother and I as a single mother. If she were here, she would no doubt say it was because she truly did get her strength to push through from the Lord.

— Allyssia Ginter, Cindy's daughter

Cindy's note

Psalm 34:8

Taste and see that the Lord is good. Oh, the joys of those who trust in him.

TRUST

Cindy's Note to Self:

Great faith in the problem or GREAT FAITH in God?

DON'T WORRY, YOU WILL EAT.

Taste and see that the Lord is good. How blessed is the one who takes shelter in him.

(Psalm 34:8)

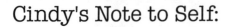

A NOTE FROM ACTIV8HER

Just like David the psalmist, Cindy had an ability to cry out to God in her times of need. She also had a way of giving him gratitude and glory when he responded. Through sheer determination, she did it with a bubbling joy. Spend a few minutes with Psalm 34:4–10. Think of a time when you have tasted and seen the goodness of God in your life and write about it as the psalmist did. Or are you in a place where you need to cry out for something? Write out your need to God.

DATE: _____ / _____ / _____   S M T W T H F S

NOTE TO SELF

Cindy's Note to Self:

If you know God owns EVERYTHING, do not worry about having ENOUGH necessities.

"Therefore I tell you, do not worry about your life, what you will eat or drink, or about your body, what you will wear. Isn't there more to life than food and more to the body than clothing? Look at the birds in the sky. They do not sow, or reap, or gather into barns, yet your heavenly Father feeds them. Aren't you more valuable than they are?"

(Matthew 6:25–26)

A NOTE FROM ACTIV8HER

Cindy was a hard worker who somehow managed to trust God would provide for her family when there seemed to be endless roadblocks. Write a prayer and ask God to help you overcome worry and, where needed, rebuild trust.

NOTE TO SELF

Cindy's Note to Self:

With JESUS on my side, I'll triumph over <u>ANY</u> trial. I'll pass that finish line with JESUS.

Happy is the one who endures testing, because when he has proven to be genuine, he will receive the crown of life that God promised to those who love him.

(James 1:12)

A NOTE FROM ACTIV8HER

Does "happy" seem like a stretch when it comes to trials and testing? If we don't trust Jesus when we endure tests and trials, we may discover bitterness rather than happiness. Cindy endured because of Jesus in her life. His faithfulness made her happy! Look back on a recent struggle in your own life and write about the reward that you saw come out of it.

DATE: _____ / _____ / _____   S M T W TH F S

NOTE TO SELF

_____
_____
_____
_____
_____
_____
_____
_____
_____
_____
_____
_____
_____
_____
_____
_____
_____
_____
_____
_____
_____
_____
_____
_____

Cindy's Note to Self:

JOSEPH was sold by his brothers to be a slave, put in prison, and <u>in one day</u> he was made prime minister of a nation. GOD HAS PURPOSE in your pain.

Now, do not be upset and do not be angry with yourselves because you sold me here, for God sent me ahead of you to preserve life! (Genesis 45:5)

A NOTE FROM ACTIV8HER

Just like Joseph, we may endure some painful experiences. And, just like Joseph, if we remain focused on God, we will discover the purpose for the pain. Have you seen the purpose from your pain yet? Ask God to give you a glimpse.

NOTE TO SELF

Cindy's Note to Self:

GOD was working on the obstacle when I was not EVEN AWARE of it. YOU don't have to see it. Just KNOW he's WORKING on it.

Keeping our eyes fixed on Jesus, the pioneer and perfecter of our faith. For the joy set out for him he endured the cross, disregarding its shame, and has taken his seat at the right hand of the throne of God.

(Hebrews 12:2)

A NOTE FROM ACTIV8HER

We can look at a situation from every side and still not have a clear picture of it. What we can be clear about is that God knows the ins and outs of it all. Write about a situation in your life that you are trying to figure out. End with the declaration that your eyes are fixed on Jesus and you know he has your good in mind.

NOTE TO SELF

Cindy's Note to Self:

You're not a PERFECT mom— you don't have perfect kids, BUT you serve a PERFECT God!!

Trust in the Lord with all your heart, and do not rely on your own understanding. Acknowledge him in all your ways, and he will make your paths straight. (Proverbs 3:5–6)

A NOTE FROM ACTIV8HER

Every time Cindy, Chrissy and I met, we'd confess our failings and fears of not enough. Then we'd offer one another the reminder that perfection was impossible, but we could trust our perfect Father. That's the promise for you, too. When you rely on your own strength you will be forced to strive for what seems beyond your reach. Acknowledge God now and ask him to make your path straight.

–Kolleen

NOTE TO SELF

Cindy's Note to Self:

Discouraged?

1. We get our focus off of GOD and onto the OBSTACLE.

2. Focus on HIS RESOURCES and PROMISES, not my power or resources.

He is your constant source of stability; he abundantly provides safety and great wisdom; he gives all this to those who fear him.

(Isaiah 33:6)

A NOTE FROM ACTIV8HER

It's easy to allow your mind to focus on the struggles of life, especially when you're tired and life keeps coming at you. In what situation are you relying on your own power and resources when you could be looking for God to provide safety and/or great wisdom?

DATE: _____ / _____ / _____   S M T W TH F S

NOTE TO SELF

Cindy's note

Elijah was sent 7 times to see if the rain was coming. Finally after doing the right thing over & over & over God moved & Deborah something happened.

OBEDIENCE

Cindy's Note to Self:

Elijah sent his servant 7 TIMES to see if the rain was coming. FINALLY, after doing the RIGHT THING over & over & over God moved & something HAPPENED.

He told his servant, "Go on up and look in the direction of the sea." So he went on up, looked, and reported, "There is nothing." Seven times Elijah sent him to look. The seventh time the servant said, "Look, a small cloud, the size of the palm of a man's hand, is rising up from the sea." (1 Kings 18:43–44)

A NOTE FROM ACTIV8HER

We may get weary of doing the right thing over and over again, but we must fight the temptation to give up! If we do, we might miss out on the move God is about to make on our behalf. What have you been waiting for?

In your prayer time, ask God to help you look up and wait patiently for his timing.

NOTE TO SELF

Cindy's Note to Self:

YOU ARE never going to be problem free so LEARN to ENJOY what Jesus died to give you—LIFE!

But the fruit of the Spirit is love, joy, peace, patience, kindness, goodness, faithfulness, gentleness, and self-control. Against such things there is no law. (Galatians 5:22–23)

A NOTE FROM ACTIV8HER

A great price was paid for you to live abundantly–the life of Jesus Christ. Craft a prayer of thanksgiving to the Father for the gift of his Son. Acknowledge the places in your life where you see the fruits of his Spirit are evident.

NOTE TO SELF

Cindy's Note to Self:

Sometimes we do the RIGHT THING, and we don't get the RIGHT RESULTS. It's never about what I'm doing— it's about what GOD'S doing.

If possible, so far as it depends on you, live peaceably with all people. (Romans 12:18)

A NOTE FROM ACTIV8HER

Cindy's note allows us to remember that we must move out of the way and just do what God is asking of us. We easily stumble into defeat when we put our expectations on what we think the outcome should be. Ask God to give you the tenacity to keep doing the right thing because he says it's the right thing.

NOTE TO SELF

Cindy's Note to Self:

The ONLY way to get free is do it AFRAID.

Then Samuel said, "Does the Lord take pleasure in burnt offerings and sacrifices as much as he does in obedience? Certainly, obedience is better than sacrifice; paying attention is better than the fat of rams."

(1 Samuel 15:22)

A NOTE FROM ACTIV8HER

Fear and other feelings can get in the way of obeying God. Cindy and today's scripture remind us that feelings need to take the backseat to obedience. Explore with the Lord what feelings might be getting in the way of your obedience.

NOTE TO SELF

Cindy's Note to Self:

It's not about how we FEEL ~ it's about how we ACT. Don't be afraid to tell God how we feel, JUST DON'T ACT how we FEEL.

If we live by the Spirit, let us also behave in accordance with the Spirit. (Galatians 5:25)

A NOTE FROM ACTIV8HER

Your feelings are indicators but don't allow them to become dictators. Tell God how you are feeling and then hand your feelings over to him. Ask him to replace the feelings with his joy and peace. When you get up, leave the feelings with him.

NOTE TO SELF

Cindy's Note to Self:

JESUS TOLD THEM: "Don't let anyone deceive you." Our children, grandchildren and great grandchildren MUST KNOW THE TRUTH in order to not be deceived in the end times.

Again, however, pay very careful attention, lest you forget the things you have seen and disregard them for the rest of your life; instead teach them to your children and grandchildren. (Deuteronomy 4:9)

A NOTE FROM ACTIV8HER

Susan Alexander Yates wrote, "The most important filter your child can have in any decision making process is the Word of God."*

Cindy's notecards had a great impact on her children's lives. Ask God for practical ways to share his Word with your children or grandchildren.

---

* *The Woman's Study Bible*, The Holy Bible, New King James Version (Nashville: Thomas Nelson, 1995). 288.

NOTE TO SELF

_____
_____
_____
_____
_____
_____
_____
_____
_____
_____
_____
_____
_____
_____
_____
_____
_____
_____
_____
_____
_____
_____
_____
_____
_____

Cindy's Note to Self:

FOCUS on God—He'll remind you that HE'S WITH YOU through this.

When you pass through the waters, I am with you; when you pass through the streams, they will not overwhelm you. When you walk through the fire, you will not be burned; the flames will not harm you.

(Isaiah 43:2)

A NOTE FROM ACTIV8HER

If God remained faithful to the Israelites, you can be sure he will remain faithful to you. Whatever you're going through—ask God to give you reminders to "look up" when you turn your focus away from him.

NOTE TO SELF

Cindy's note

love is all about how we treat people especially when theres nothing they can do in return for you.

GENEROSITY

Cindy's Note to Self:

LOVE is about how we TREAT PEOPLE. Especially when there's NOTHING they can do in return for you.

But love your enemies, and do good, and lend, expecting nothing back. Then your reward will be great, and you will be sons of the Most High, because he is kind to ungrateful and evil people.

(Luke 6:35)

A NOTE FROM ACTIV8HER

Jesus never sought revenge, and while we might grumble when discussing our irritations, we must always come back to this truth: Loving others like Jesus means we allow his love to flow through us. How does God want you to reveal his love to others this week through you?

NOTE TO SELF

Cindy's Note to Self:

Christian hospitality differs from social entertainment. ENTERTAINING focuses on the host. The home must be spotless; the food must be WELL PREPARED and ABUNDANT. The host must appear relaxed and good-natured. HOSPITALITY, by contrast, focuses on the GUESTS' needs, such as a place to stay, nourishing food, a listening ear, or just acceptance.

Show hospitality
to one another
without complaining.
(1 Peter 4:9)

A NOTE FROM ACTIV8HER

Genuine generosity and genuine hospitality are similar in that neither is done for personal gain. As you read Cindy's note, does it bring up an inner struggle of your own? What could be the root of that? Explore this with the Lord.

NOTE TO SELF

Cindy's Note to Self:

Hospitality CAN HAPPEN in a messy house. It CAN HAPPEN around a dinner table where the main dish is canned soup. DON'T HESITATE to offer HOSPITALITY just because you are too tired, too busy or not wealthy enough to entertain.

Contribute to the needs of the saints, pursue hospitality.

(Romans 12:13)

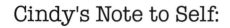

A NOTE FROM ACTIV8HER

Cindy overcame a "poverty mind-set" and amazed us with her gift of generosity. Don't allow excuses (or insecurity) of your "lack" to take away the joy you'll receive when you invite people over! Share yourself and what the Lord has provided with others. With whom do you pursue hospitality? Would you prayerfully confront fear and then surrender all your "stuff" to God?

DATE: _____ / _____ / _____   S M T W TH F S

NOTE TO SELF

Cindy's Note to Self:

LOVE IS directed OUTWARD toward others, not inward toward self. God helps us SET ASIDE our own natural DESIRES so that we can LOVE and NOT EXPECT anything in return.

"By all these things, I have shown you that by working in this way we must help the weak, and remember the words of the Lord Jesus that he himself said, 'It is more blessed to give than to receive.'"

(Acts 20:35)

A NOTE FROM ACTIV8HER

Cindy was a wonderful giver! She was very creative in her ways of blessing those around her. Generous gifts are not always tangible and are to be given with no expectation of there being a return. Who can you bless today with no expectation of anything in return?

NOTE TO SELF

Cindy's Note to Self:

A GODLY heritage is worth much MORE THAN a HERITAGE of wealthy people.

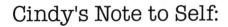

Better is little with the fear of the Lord than great wealth and turmoil with it. (Proverbs 15:16)

A NOTE FROM ACTIV8HER

Cindy was diligent to protect herself from the green eyes of envy. Rather than live a life of striving and turmoil she was intentional about mastering the desire for wealth.

If greed has a grip on your heart, ask God to help you grow into a content person and help raise the next generation in his principles so they can learn this, too.

DATE: _____ / _____ / _____   S M T W TH F S

NOTE TO SELF

_____
_____
_____
_____
_____
_____
_____
_____
_____
_____
_____
_____
_____
_____
_____
_____
_____
_____
_____
_____
_____
_____
_____
_____
_____
_____

Cindy's Note to Self:

Kingdom DWELLER or Kingdom BUILDER.

We are coworkers
belonging to God.
You are God's field,
God's building.
(1 Corinthians 3:9)

A NOTE FROM ACTIV8HER

Kingdom builders have a role to play. There was a day that Cindy realized the difference between being a kingdom dweller and a kingdom builder. It was the day she realized she could serve God by answering the call to serve in her church. Do you see yourself as a builder of God's kingdom? If you haven't thought about that before now, how can you move from dweller to builder?

DATE: _____ / _____ / _____   S M T W TH F S

NOTE TO SELF

Cindy's Note to Self:

God picked me out as HIS OWN and ADOPTED me.

He did this by predestining us to adoption as his legal heirs through Jesus Christ, according to the pleasure of his will—to the praise of the glory of his grace that he has freely bestowed on us in his dearly loved Son.

(Ephesians 1:5–6)

A NOTE FROM ACTIV8HER

Have you ever considered how much joy it brings to our heavenly Father to hear his daughters acknowledge who they rightfully belong to? If you don't have a deep revelation of your true identity in Christ, ask him to reveal this aspect of identity to you. It's time to live as his adopted daughter and receive the fullness of his inheritance!

NOTE TO SELF

Cindy's note

get over anger
quickly. for when
you are angry
you give a mighty
foothold to the Eph 4:26
devil

FORGIVENESS

Cindy's Note to Self:

Get over anger QUICKLY. For when you are angry you give a MIGHTY FOOTHOLD to the devil.

Be angry and do not sin; do not let the sun go down on the cause of your anger.
(Ephesians 4:26)

A NOTE FROM ACTIV8HER

Anger is destructive. We surrendered many emotions and attitudes while sitting at the kitchen table together as we talked through our emotions. Is it possible to let go of anger before the sun goes down? We discovered the answer was absolutely – if you really wanted to. Be honest with your anger. What are you mad about? Tell God and as you write out your anger imagine he lifts it off the pages right before your eyes.

DATE: _____ / _____ / _____   S M T W TH F S

NOTE TO SELF

Cindy's Note to Self:

Hatred and bitterness are LIFE WEEDS with long roots that grow in the heart and corrupt all of life. If the mere mention of someone's name provokes you to anger, CONFESS your BITTERNESS as sin. If bitterness is not COMPLETELY REMOVED, it will grow back, making matters worse.

Now Haman went forth that day pleased and very much encouraged. But when Haman saw Mordecai at the king's gate, and he did not rise or tremble in his presence, Haman was filled with rage toward Mordecai.

(Esther 5:9)

A NOTE FROM ACTIV8HER

Anger, rage, hatred, bitterness–these are big emotions with dangerous consequences. Haman's bitterness led him to die on gallows he had built to kill Mordecai. Is there a name that comes to your mind that brings up feelings of bitterness or worse? Confess it now as sin and ask God to help you pull that root before it goes deeper.

NOTE TO SELF

Cindy's Note to Self:

Peter asked Jesus: HOW MANY times do I have to FORGIVE someone because he was having a hard time with one of the disciples and Jesus gave him, 7X70 which just means a PERFECT NUMBER. However many times it takes.

Then Peter came to him and said, "Lord, how many times must I forgive my brother who sins against me? As many as seven times?" Jesus said to him, "Not seven times, I tell you, but seventy-seven times!" (Matthew 18:21–22)

A NOTE FROM ACTIV8HER

We don't know who Peter was having a hard time forgiving, but no doubt we can relate to his question. We would miss out on so much if we refused to forgive one another. Who do you need to forgive? Who do you need to release from the prison of your heart? Jesus forgave; we can, too. Let God lead you in a prayer of release today.

DATE: _____ / _____ / _____   S M T W TH F S

NOTE TO SELF

Cindy's Note to Self:

I'm starting a FRESH and a NEW day. I'm forgiving the people who've hurt me. I'm RELEASING and letting go of bitterness. Letting go of any grudges. I'm not gonna hold on to any of that. I'm just gonna MOVE ON AND LIVE my life free.

Do not judge, and you will not be judged; do not condemn, and you will not be condemned; forgive, and you will be forgiven.
(Luke 6:37)

A NOTE FROM ACTIV8HER

I can almost hear Cindy's voice declaring this now and it sounds like the voice of freedom! Think of the work you have done with the Lord in the past few days. Read Cindy's note out loud. Write about the sense of freedom you are experiencing.

–Chrissy

DATE: _____ / _____ / _____   S M T W TH F S

NOTE TO SELF

Cindy's Note to Self:

Don't have SELECTIVE HEARING with God.

My sheep listen to my voice, and I know them, and they follow me.
(John 10:27)

A NOTE FROM ACTIV8HER

This brings a smile to my face when I remember Cindy putting her finger in her ears and declaring, "What? I can't hear you" when God revealed a hard truth of understanding. Sheep follow the shepherd during every difficulty with confidence that he is the one they can trust. Spend your prayer time today asking Jesus to become your personal shepherd. Can you trust him to lead you?

–Kolleen

NOTE TO SELF

Cindy's Note to Self:

The enemy will not show you HOW FAR you've come ~ only how far you have to go. DO NOT feel guilty or bad when you are tempted, ONLY when you give in to temptation.

No trial has overtaken you that is not faced by others. And God is faithful: He will not let you be tried beyond what you are able to bear, but with the trial will also provide a way out so that you may be able to endure it.

(1 Corinthians 10:13)

A NOTE FROM ACTIV8HER

The enemy loves to pull back his fiery dart and release it with his accusations of failure. He wants you to believe you failed when tempted, but that's not what God says. He has a plan for our escape from temptation. What is tempting you now? God knows which key will open the door that leads to the escape route. Write down the plan as he instructs you.

NOTE TO SELF

Cindy's Note to Self:

Their stupidity is NOT going to CONTROL me.

Do not be overcome by evil, but overcome evil with good.
(Romans 12:21)

A NOTE FROM ACTIV8HER

If Cindy let someone mistreat her or lead her down a wrong thought path once, you can be sure it was not likely to happen again. But it wasn't revenge she was looking for. She simply made the choice to not let their actions control her. Then she reset her sight on the right path. Is there someone whose stupidity has control over you? Recognize it now and ask God to help you choose a new way to act or think.

DATE: _____ / _____ / _____   S M T W TH F S

NOTE TO SELF

Cindy's note

I'm not going to eat the poison of letting myself get offended and staying there I'm going to give mercy and assume they did not mean to hurt me.

MERCY

Cindy's Note to Self:

I'm **NOT GOING TO** eat the poison of letting myself get offended and staying there. I'm **GOING TO** give **MERCY** and assume they *did not mean to hurt me.*

Be merciful, just as your Father is merciful.
(Luke 6:36)

A NOTE FROM ACTIV8HER

If you have a spirit of offense everything you hear will filter through that lens and distort how you hear what's being said. God wants to break that from his daughters so they can offer the same mercy to others that he offers to them. Let this be your prayer focus today. A release from a spirit of offense.

DATE: _____ / _____ / _____   S M T W TH F S

NOTE TO SELF

Cindy's Note to Self:

Do life's problems always seem to go from bad to worse? GOD is THE ONLY ONE who can reverse this downward spiral. He can take our problems and turn them into GLORIOUS VICTORIES. There is one necessary requirement—We, like David, must CRY OUT, "Turn to me and have mercy on me." When we are willing to do that GOD CAN turn the worst into SOMETHING WONDERFUL. The NEXT STEP is yours; God has already made his offer.

Turn toward me and have mercy on me, for I am alone and oppressed. Deliver me from my distress; rescue me from my suffering.

(Psalm 25:16–17)

A NOTE FROM ACTIV8HER

The offer is on the table. Is there a situation that is seemingly going from bad to worse? Write a prayer calling on God's mercy. Leave space so in the days ahead you can come back and write the testimony of his rescue.

NOTE TO SELF

_____
_____
_____
_____
_____
_____
_____
_____
_____
_____
_____
_____
_____
_____
_____
_____
_____
_____
_____
_____
_____
_____
_____
_____
_____
_____
_____

Cindy's Note to Self:

"May the GOD OF HOPE fill you with all JOY and PEACE as you TRUST IN HIM, so that you may overflow with hope by the POWER of the Holy Spirit" (Romans 13:13, NIV).

But Jesus did not permit him to do so. Instead, he said to him, "Go to your home and to your people and tell them what the Lord has done for you, that he had mercy on you."

(Mark 5:19)

A NOTE FROM ACTIV8HER

Understanding mercy is one of God's character traits that will enable us to maintain a heart of joy, peace, and trust. Does his mercy flow from your heart to others? Do a word study and write what you discover about the mercy of God.

NOTE TO SELF

Cindy's Note to Self:

God's PLANS for me and my children are NOT TO harm us but to PROSPER us.

"'For I know what I have planned for you,' says the Lord. 'I have plans to prosper you, not to harm you. I have plans to give you a future filled with hope.'"
(Jeremiah 29:11)

A NOTE FROM ACTIV8HER

There were moments in Cindy's walk with God when she clung to this verse as circumstances caused her to want to waver. Are there times in your life when you have had to do the same? Are there circumstances in your life today over which you need to make this declaration?

NOTE TO SELF

_____
_____
_____
_____
_____
_____
_____
_____
_____
_____
_____
_____
_____
_____
_____
_____
_____
_____
_____
_____
_____
_____
_____
_____
_____
_____

Cindy's Note to Self:

Be excited WHERE YOU ARE, not always beating yourself up for your flaws. How much of TODAY are you losing because you're holding on to YESTERDAY'S sins?

So then, if anyone is in Christ, he is a new creation; what is old has passed away—look, what is new has come!

(2 Corinthians 5:17)

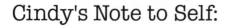

A NOTE FROM ACTIV8HER

Rather than miss today's joys because of all that irritated you yesterday, hand those irritations over to Jesus. Give yourself some grace as you become the new–to–you creation he's always known you as. You might stumble but he will lift you up. Make today's prayer one of gratitude for who you are becoming.

NOTE TO SELF

Cindy's Note to Self:

Focus on your POTENTIAL NOT your FAULTS.

And we all, with unveiled faces reflecting the glory of the Lord, are being transformed into the same image from one degree of glory to another, which is from the Lord, who is the Spirit.
(2 Corinthians 3:18)

A NOTE FROM ACTIV8HER

We are all great works in progress— IN PROGRESS! List three things you see as faults in yourself. Then list six areas of potential in your life. End your time by thanking God that you are still a work in progress, and he is bringing you from one degree of glory to another.

NOTE TO SELF

Cindy's Note to Self:

You don't have to be under the stress of PERFECTIONISM. Perfectionism gives you MAXIMUM anxiety.

Come to me, all you who are weary and burdened, and I will give you rest. (Matthew 11:28)

A NOTE FROM ACTIV8HER

One of my favorite memories of our Bible study together were the reminders we gave to one another that God never sought perfection, but in Christ we had great potential. Do you struggle with perfectionism? That's a heavy burden to carry. Give that weight to Jesus and accept his rest.

–Kolleen

NOTE TO SELF

Cindy's note

Be determined to get the VERY BEST God has for you

PRESS ON !

DISCIPLINE

Cindy's Note to Self:

Be determined to get the <u>VERY BEST</u> God has for you. <u>PRESS ON!</u>

And I pray this, that your love may abound even more and more in knowledge and every kind of insight so that you can decide what is best, and thus be sincere and blameless for the day of Christ. (Philippians 1:9–10)

A NOTE FROM ACTIV8HER

There was a day when Cindy became determined she would not settle for less than God's best. She did this by asking for mentors that would (1) pray with her and (2) help her recognize if comfort was prohibiting her ability to press on. What is holding you back? How you were raised? A victim mindset of negativity? Use Paul's prayer as your outline and make it personal for you today.

NOTE TO SELF

Cindy's Note to Self:

RESIST the devil.
Don't ACT like him.

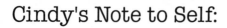

So submit to God. But resist the devil and he will flee from you. Draw near to God and he will draw near to you. Cleanse your hands, you sinners, and make your hearts pure, you double-minded.

(James 4:7–8)

A NOTE FROM ACTIV8HER

This is such a Cindy statement! It is so easy to get sucked into acting like the devil. But James gives us clear and direct advice. Resist the devil and draw near to God. Draw near to God as you write to Him about an area that you are working to resist the devil.

DATE: _____ / _____ / _____   S M T W TH F S

NOTE TO SELF

Cindy's Note to Self:

Where you let your THOUGHTS go that's where your LIFE goes—as a man THINKETH so he becomes.

For those who live according to the flesh have their outlook shaped by the things of the flesh, but those who live according to the Spirit have their outlook shaped by the things of the Spirit.

(Romans 8:5)

A NOTE FROM ACTIV8HER

Don't be surprised by the devil's attempts to take your thoughts places they should not go. God intends for us to live with a kingdom mindset—no longer trapped by the ideals of the culture around us. Cindy understood that allowing her flesh to lead her meant a different outcome than what she longed for in Christ. What are you allowing to shape your outlook?

NOTE TO SELF

Cindy's Note to Self:

Do what is EXCELLENT–holy THOUGHTS, holy behavior.

Finally, brothers and sisters, whatever is true, whatever is worthy of respect, whatever is just, whatever is pure, whatever is lovely, whatever is commendable, if something is excellent or praiseworthy, think about these things. (Philippians 4:8)

A NOTE FROM ACTIV8HER

The way we behave is a result of the way we think. Cindy, as well as Paul, the author of the letter to the Philippians, understood this. What is a behavior in your life that you would like to see transformed? Is it a result of unholy thinking? How can you change what you think to bring a change in your behavior?

NOTE TO SELF

Cindy's Note to Self:

THINKING the right thoughts takes PRACTICE.

Like obedient children, do not comply with the evil urges you used to follow in your ignorance, but, like the Holy One who called you, become holy yourselves in all of your conduct, for it is written, "You shall be holy, because I am holy."

(1 Peter 1:14–16)

A NOTE FROM ACTIV8HER

Cindy's note cards that were placed throughout her home, in her car, and busting out of her Bible were a discipline she employed that helped her change her thought patterns. Do you have disciplines in your life that help you renew your mind?

NOTE TO SELF

_____
_____
_____
_____
_____
_____
_____
_____
_____
_____
_____
_____
_____
_____
_____
_____
_____
_____
_____
_____
_____
_____
_____
_____
_____

Cindy's Note to Self:

Neglect the NEGATIVE THOUGHTS until they starve to death. This process takes PERSEVERANCE.

Keep thinking about things above, not things on the earth, for you have died and your life is hidden with Christ in God.
(Colossians 3:2–3)

A NOTE FROM ACTIV8HER

To persevere* is to continue to do or achieve something despite difficulty or even failure. It takes effort and determination to reroute those thought patterns from negative to positive. What is a negative thought of yours that you'd like to see starved to death? Rewrite that thought from the perspective of your identity that is now hidden in Christ.

* *Merriam-Webster.com Dictionary*, s.v. "perseverance," accessed September 24, 2023, https://www.merriam-webster.com/dictionary/perseverance.

DATE: _____ / _____ / _____   S M T W TH F S

NOTE TO SELF

Cindy's Note to Self:

Get up EARLY and make a DEPOSIT in your generation's lives. Spend time WITH GOD.

Now all discipline seems painful at the time, not joyful. But later it produces the fruit of peace and righteousness for those trained by it. (Hebrews 12:11)

A NOTE FROM ACTIV8HER

Oh, we see the fruit of this in Cindy's life! She warred for her children and even her grandchildren before they were born. Waking up a little earlier or staying up a little later is painful at the time. The promise though, is peace and righteousness. Use this time and space to make a deposit into your generations to come.

NOTE TO SELF

Cindy's note

I'm not where
I want to
be but thank
God I'm not where
I used to be

SPIRITUAL GROWTH

Cindy's Note to Self:

I'm not where I want to be but THANK GOD I'm not where I USED TO BE.

Do not be conformed to this present world, but be transformed by the renewing of your mind, so that you may test and approve what is the will of God— what is good and well-pleasing and perfect.
(Romans 12:2)

A NOTE FROM ACTIV8HER

Thanks for the reminder, Cindy! Transformation takes time; in fact, it is a life-long process. Refuse to allow the messy moments to keep you from pressing forward into growth ones. God transforms people through the power of his Word. Take the time today to thank him for the transformation taking place in your life right now!

NOTE TO SELF

Cindy's Note to Self:

Don't you REALIZE you are paying for your sin and I ALREADY did that? Get OVER IT and MOVE ON. You are NOT VALUABLE to me in this condition.

But they are justified freely by his grace through the redemption that is in Christ Jesus. God publicly displayed him at his death as the mercy seat accessible through faith.

(Romans 3:24)

A NOTE FROM ACTIV8HER

Cindy would say, "Duhhh!" to this reminder. Jesus Christ has paid for your sin—once and for all time. What things from your past are you feeling the need to still pay for? Thank Jesus now for paying the price for those things. End your time by writing out the words, PAID IN FULL!

NOTE TO SELF

Cindy's Note to Self:

MANAGING your time is something you learn. Teach me to MAKE THE MOST of my time so that I will GROW in WISDOM.

So teach us to number our days, that we may gain a heart of wisdom. (Psalm 90:12 NKJV)

A NOTE FROM ACTIV8HER

As a single mom, it could be extremely difficult for Cindy to manage work life, home life, and spiritual life. So, she learned the importance of making the most of the time God had given to her. Our conversations during her last days recounted the memories of special moments of time spent. Are you spending your time wisely? Perhaps today's prayer could be asking the Lord to show you.

DATE: _____ / _____ / _____   S M T W TH F S

NOTE TO SELF

Cindy's Note to Self:

Remember the GOODNESS & PROMISES of God. LET THE WORD wash you of the discouragement. Remembrance PROVOKES PRAISE and sets up a domino effect. Command your mind to SUBMIT to the way of God.

When I remember these things, I pour out my soul within me. For I used to go with the multitude; I went with them to the house of God, With the voice of joy and praise, With a multitude that kept a pilgrim feast. (Psalm 42:4 NKJV)

A NOTE FROM ACTIV8HER

We grow in our faith every single time we choose to remember the goodness and promises of God. Rather than allow discouragement to drown you use this time in the Word to remember. Begin to praise and let the Spirit wash discouragement away.

NOTE TO SELF

Cindy's Note to Self:

Ask the Lord every day to make you MORE and MORE like Jesus. As he becomes a STRONGER and STRONGER foundation of your life, your eyes will begin to move away from yourself and toward your TRUE FOCUS: your heavenly Father.

I have been crucified with Christ, and it is no longer I who live, but Christ lives in me. So the life I now live in the body, I live because of the faithfulness of the Son of God, who loved me and gave himself for me.

(Galatians 2:20)

A NOTE FROM ACTIV8HER

In Christ, you are now a citizen of his kingdom. Let today's prayer flow from a heart of gratitude and love for your King. If you have lost sight of the magnitude of his love for you, allow him to envelope you and reveal his heart of love to you.

DATE: _____ / _____ / _____   S M T W TH F S

NOTE TO SELF

Cindy's Note to Self:

God looks for
STEADY GROWTH,
NOT instant perfection.

Not that I have already attained this—that is, I have not already been perfected—but I strive to lay hold of that for which Christ Jesus also laid hold of me. (Philippians 3:12)

A NOTE FROM ACTIV8HER

Understanding that God doesn't demand instant perfection is a freeing thought. But it doesn't let us off the hook. Following Paul's (and Cindy's) example, we are to be determined in our pursuit of progress. Do you have a tendency toward perfectionism? Take a few moments to thank God for the progress you have made and make a recommitment to keep moving toward the goal of Christ's example.

NOTE TO SELF

Cindy's Note to Self:

It's the DEEP and DIFFICULT places that cause us to GROW, and it's in the good times we get to enjoy the growth we've gained from the difficult times.

During his earthly life Christ offered both requests and supplications, with loud cries and tears, to the one who was able to save him from death and he was heard because of his devotion.

(Hebrews 5:7)

A NOTE FROM ACTIV8HER

We are grateful to have walked with one another for 20+ years of highs and lows. Sometimes steady; sometimes not-so-much. Through the years we were able to look back and take note of the changes God was making in each one of us that carried us into the next set of circumstances. Who walks beside you when you're in a deep and difficult place? Where can you say growth has taken place in you?

NOTE TO SELF

Cindy's note

I'm not going to eat the <u>POISON</u> of letting myself get offended and staying there. I'm not going to let what they SAID hurt me anymore LET IT GO

RELATIONSHIPS

Cindy's Note to Self:

I'm NOT GOING to eat the <u>poison</u> of letting myself get <u>OFFENDED</u> and STAYING there. I'm NOT going to let what they said hurt me anymore. LET IT GO.

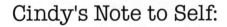

Whenever you stand praying, if you have anything against anyone, forgive him, so that your Father in heaven will also forgive you your sins.

(Mark 11:25)

A NOTE FROM ACTIV8HER

Cindy was like many other women who carry some exceptionally deep wounds. This card is a reminder to each one who reads it of how poisonous offense becomes when we allow it to fester. We must choose to forgive. We do this for our benefit, not theirs. Then we release the offense and the offender. Are you holding on to an offense? Who comes to mind? Journal your way to freedom.

NOTE TO SELF

Cindy's Note to Self:

I never have to be sad when I am not "invited" because I ALREADY received the best invitation of ALL. God—"and HE IS THE ONE who invited you into this wonderful friendship with HIS SON, JESUS CHRIST our Lord" (1 Corinthians 1:9).

God is faithful, by whom you were called into fellowship with his son, Jesus Christ our Lord. (1 Corinthians 1:9)

A NOTE FROM ACTIV8HER

It never feels good to not be invited, but Cindy's reminder that we've already received the best invitation refocuses our perspective.

Are you holding grudges for the times you've been left off the list? Can you turn your grudge into a prayer of thanks for God's invitation?

NOTE TO SELF

Cindy's Note to Self:

Words are POWERFUL, and how you use them reflects on your RELATIONSHIP with God.

Lord, who may be a guest in your home? Who may live on your holy hill? Whoever lives a blameless life,

does what is right,

and speaks honestly.

He does not slander,

or do harm to others

or insult his neighbor.

(Psalm 15:1–3)

A NOTE FROM ACTIV8HER

Our relationship with God is the foundation of our relationship with others. When we are in fellowship with God it shows in the way we speak and deal with one another. Look up some scriptures about the power of our tongues and words. Write them here and work to commit them to memory.

NOTE TO SELF

Cindy's Note to Self:

Hurts. You CAN CHOOSE, like many, to chain yourself to your hurt... Or you can choose like some, to PUT AWAY YOUR HURTS before they become hates...How does God deal with your bitter heart? He reminds you that what you have is MORE IMPORTANT than what you don't have. You still have your relationship with God and NO ONE CAN TAKE THAT.

See to it that no one comes short of the grace of God, that no one be like a bitter root springing up and causing trouble, and through it many become defiled.

(Hebrews 12:15)

A NOTE FROM ACTIV8HER

We can't allow the stinger of a hurt to remain. Removing it quickly extracts any poison that leads to infection; which, if not taken care of quickly, can lead to death.

During our study times together, we held one another accountable to this and did many "heart checks."

When have you allowed a hurt to fester? What was the consequence? Are you hurt or did a hurt turn into hate? Give it to God—today.

NOTE TO SELF

Cindy's Note to Self:

The EASIEST TIME to get rid of an offense is when you first feel it. It is a small seed, and it will have no soil to grow ROOTS. But if you keep talking and thinking about it, you grow BITTERNESS.

A person's wisdom has made him slow to anger, and it is his glory to overlook an offense.
(Proverbs 19:11)

A NOTE FROM ACTIV8HER

We want good seeds to go deep into rich soil. But the seed of offense has no place in our garden. Self-discipline will take the thought of offense captive and give it no place to grow. Pray for God to help you have the ability to shrug off offenses before they take root.

NOTE TO SELF

Cindy's Note to Self:

Don't suck the LIFE out of your friends by spending ALL YOUR TIME murmuring and complaining.

Pleasant words are like a honeycomb, sweet to the soul and healing to the bones. (Proverbs 16:24)

A NOTE FROM ACTIV8HER

Ha! This is a great word, Cindy! I can hear her say: "Ain't nobody got time to listen to that!" Are you a complainer? If you're ready to change, God will show you how to break the cycle of negative thinking and speaking. Ask him to open your ears and help you hear how you sound in the ears of others. Make this your prayer today.

–Kolleen

NOTE TO SELF

Cindy's Note to Self:

It DOES NOT increase your value when you find you can do something that NOBODY ELSE you know can do. Nor does it decrease your value when you are with people who CAN DO THINGS that you cannot do.

For we are his creative work, having been created in Christ Jesus for good works that God prepared beforehand so we can do them. (Ephesians 2:10)

A NOTE FROM ACTIV8HER

You were created for some specific and unique purposes in the kingdom of God. The people around you were created uniquely for their own. We are not supposed to be the same, so why do we compare ourselves to others? Is this a struggle for you? Can you find freedom in these truths today?

NOTE TO SELF

Cindy's note

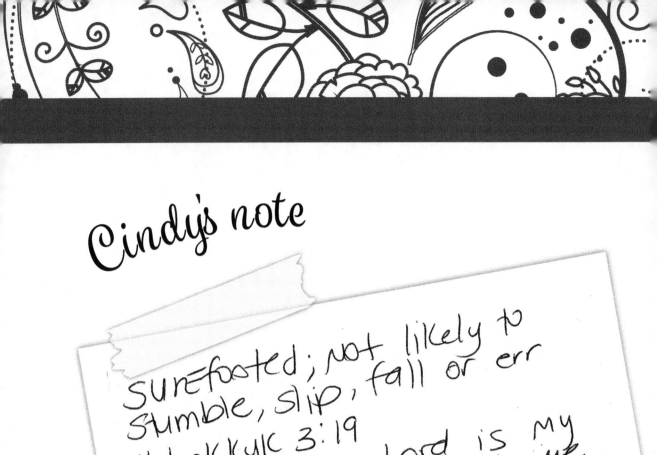

Surefooted; not likely to
stumble, slip, fall or err
Habakkuk 3:19
The sovereign Lord is my
strength! He will make me
as surefooted as a deer and
bring me safely over the
mountains
right now my mountain:
new job new home

FAITH

Cindy's Note to Self:

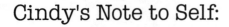

Surefooted: not likely to stumble, slip, fall or err.
The SOVEREIGN LORD is my STRENGTH!
He will make me SUREFOOTED as a deer
and bring me SAFELY over the mountains.
Right now my mountain: new job, new home.

The Sovereign LORD is my source of strength. He gives me the agility of a deer; he enables me to negotiate the rugged terrain.

(Habakkuk 3:19)

A NOTE FROM ACTIV8HER

Cindy's mountains when she wrote this note were a new job and a new home. What mountain are you facing today? God's strength is available for the climb. He is there and knows every step that needs to be taken. Explore with him today what your next steps are in your climb. Don't forget to thank him for walking with you and for giving you his strength.

NOTE TO SELF

Cindy's Note to Self:

You can EITHER worry yourself to death OR you can TRUST God to provide.

And which of you by worrying can add even one hour to his life?

(Matthew 6:27)

A NOTE FROM ACTIV8HER

Worry produces rotten fruit. It steals peace and joy from you. Cindy's notes were throughout her house as reminders that she was not in the battle alone. They were part of the toolkit she used to fight the stronghold of worry. She recognized it was a thief. Perhaps you can begin placing your own notecards in strategic spaces and places to remind you of this, too.

DATE: _____ / _____ / _____   S M T W TH F S

NOTE TO SELF

Cindy's Note to Self:

Sometimes FAITH is the absence of fear. Other times faith may be CHOOSING to BELIEVE God when your heart is melting with fear.

There is no fear in love, but perfect love drives out fear, because fear has to do with punishment. The one who fears punishment has not been perfected in love.

(1 John 4:18)

A NOTE FROM ACTIV8HER

Fear is very real and a favorite tactic of our enemy. But faith is so much bigger than fear! Cindy reminds us today that we can put our faith over our fears. It is often just a decision to move ahead despite the fear. What fear holds you back today? Decide to put your faith over that fear by asking God to help you to do it afraid.

NOTE TO SELF

Cindy's Note to Self:

God does not love us less when He gives us fewer evidences. He simply desires to GROW US UP and TEACH us to walk by faith and not by sight. These steps are most challenging when we're delivered THROUGH frightening experiences rather than FROM them.

But he said to them, "Why are you cowardly, you people of little faith?" Then he got up and rebuked the winds and the sea, and it was dead calm. (Matthew 8:26)

A NOTE FROM ACTIV8HER

Jesus knew when they stepped into the boat that they would encounter a storm. He could have told them what was coming to prepare them for the experience. He did not. He did, however, ask why they lacked faith knowing that he was in the boat with them. When you are in a storm, it is imperative that you silence the lie that God is not with you. What storm has you clinging to him today? Pray for evidence that he is with you as you walk by faith through it.

NOTE TO SELF

Cindy's Note to Self:

Hasn't **God** brought you through some **REALLY HARD** times? What makes you think he can't **BRING YOU THROUGH** this time?

For the righteousness of God is revealed in the gospel from faith to faith, just as it is written, "The righteous by faith will live." (Romans 1:17).

A NOTE FROM ACTIV8HER

In the midst of hard times, it is helpful to pause and look at God's faithfulness to us in the past. It builds our faith and helps us to make a stand in our current hardship. What are one or two instances you can recall of God's faithfulness in your past times of struggle?

NOTE TO SELF

Cindy's Note to Self:

When you can't see HIS HAND— trust HIS HEART. He sees the master plan.

He did not waver in unbelief about the promise of God but was strengthened in faith, giving glory to God. He was fully convinced that what God promised he was also able to do.
(Romans 4:20–21)

A NOTE FROM ACTIV8HER

As a single mom, Cindy had many opportunities to trust God's heart, for herself and her children. When presented with a struggle you can bet she was going to stand firm and fix her eyes on Jesus. What about you? Where are your eyes fixed?

NOTE TO SELF

Cindy's Note to Self:

When fear comes against you DON'T RUN. No one said you couldn't do it afraid.

Therefore, since we are surrounded by such a great cloud of witnesses, we must get rid of every weight and the sin that clings so closely, and run with endurance the race set out for us, keeping our eyes fixed on Jesus, the pioneer and perfecter of our faith.

(Hebrews 12:1-2)

A NOTE FROM ACTIV8HER

Cindy was not one to back away from a challenge. She took on problems with the determination and the steady pace of a long-distance runner. Fear is one thing that she had to shake off along the way. Does fear hold you back from running the race with a steady gait? Maybe there are other sins that are blurring your focus. Ask God to show you and if there is, confess it. If there isn't, thank him and ask him to help you continue to keep your eyes on Jesus.

NOTE TO SELF

Cindy's note

God probably does not enjoy humbling us any more than we enjoy being humbled, but pride is so crippling to the believer that He often has little choice.

HUMILITY

Cindy's Note to Self:

God probably does NOT ENJOY humbling us any more than we enjoy BEING HUMBLED. But PRIDE is so crippling to the believer that HE OFTEN has little choice.

Before destruction the heart of a person is proud, but humility comes before honor. (Proverbs 18:12)

A NOTE FROM ACTIV8HER

Sure, there were moments when pride snuck into our heart. But, over the years we had cultivated such trust through our friendship with one another, that we were willing to hear when pride was pointed out. Pride limits how God can use us because he hates it. Don't be afraid to allow your friends to show you where they see pride in your life. Falls hurt. When have you experienced the pain of pride? Write your own note to self as a reminder of what can be lost if pride enters.

NOTE TO SELF

Cindy's Note to Self:

Behave your way to SUCCESS.

Instead of being motivated by selfish ambition or vanity, each of you should, in humility, be moved to treat one another as more important than yourself.
(Philippians 2:3)

A NOTE FROM ACTIV8HER

According to Merriam-Webster, success is defined as a favorable or desired outcome.* That's a rather broad definition. Can you craft your own definition of success based on today's scripture? Looking at various Bible translations might add to your understanding.

* "Success." Merriam-Webster.com Dictionary, Merriam-Webster, https://www.merriam-webster.com/dictionary/success. Accessed 4 Sep. 2023.

NOTE TO SELF

Cindy's Note to Self:

Our very EXISTENCE depends on our Creator. Keeping this in perspective removes ANY TEMPTATION to have pride in personal achievement.

For by the grace given to me I say to every one of you not to think more highly of yourself than you ought to think, but to think with sober discernment, as God has distributed to each of you a measure of faith.

(Romans 12:3)

A NOTE FROM ACTIV8HER

Remember this: God chose you first, you did not find him. All that you are and all that you have come from him. Cindy was consistent to share how God was moving in her life and put the focus on him rather than herself. Who do you boast about? God or self?

DATE: _____ / _____ / _____   S M T W TH F S

NOTE TO SELF

Cindy's Note to Self:

Will this issue REALLY MATTER ten minutes from now?

But avoid foolish controversies, genealogies, quarrels, and fights about the law, because they are useless and empty.

(Titus 3:9)

A NOTE FROM ACTIV8HER

To allow humility to become part of our nature, it requires we ask the question Cindy asked. If the goal is to live like Christ and further the gospel, there will be times when it is more beneficial to move on without engaging in foolishness or quarreling. Think of a situation when you would have served the Lord better by not engaging in a foolish argument. Now, ask God to help you be conscious of when to engage and when to be still.

NOTE TO SELF

Cindy's Note to Self:

Calm mothers don't KEEP TRACK of MISTAKES and they don't punish themselves EITHER.

The LORD's loyal kindness never ceases; his compassions never end. They are fresh every morning; your faithfulness is abundant! (Lamentations 3:22–23)

A NOTE FROM ACTIV8HER

If we don't deal with regret, it will lead us to self-incrimination and defeat. Every day we have "do-over" opportunities and every day we can count on the Lord's loyal kindnesses. Receive his compassionate care for you every day. Thank him for his nature of love. Write a note to self as a reminder that regret only leads to harm.

NOTE TO SELF

Cindy's Note to Self:

One VULNERABLE PLACE we can be as a single woman, or a single parent is to FEAR not having someone to take care of us. We must let (ask) HIM TO HEAL this part of us so we won't be vulnerable to unhealthy relationships.

And God will exalt you in due time, if you humble yourselves under his mighty hand by casting all your cares on him because he cares for you.

(1 Peter 5:6–7)

A NOTE FROM ACTIV8HER

Cindy gives us wise advice today. Whether we are single or married, God is our ultimate provider. Where are the areas in your life that you are seeking care from someone other than God? What do you need? Have you opened yourself up to unhealthy vulnerability? Let today be the day you allow God to heal that part of you.

NOTE TO SELF

Cindy's Note to Self:

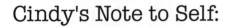

Sometimes the HARDEST PART of learning something NEW is UNLEARNING the old way of doing it.

Every scripture is inspired by God and useful for teaching, for reproof, for correction, and for training in righteousness, that the person dedicated to God may be capable and equipped for every good work.
(2 Timothy 3:16–17)

A NOTE FROM ACTIV8HER

"If you always do what you've always done you will always get what you've always got." * Cindy had a revelation that God's desire for her and her children was for good. She also recognized that to experience this good, she'd need to relearn and unlearn. She did this by allowing God's Word to reveal her new nature. What about you? What habits does God want you to unlearn so you can learn how to live in your new identity?

*https://quoteinvestigator.com/2016/04/25/get/

NOTE TO SELF

Cindy's note

Isaiah 40:31
But they that wait upon
the Lord shall renew their
strength; They shall mount
up with wings as eagles;
they shall run, an not
be weary; and they shall
walk, and not faint.

STRENGTH

Cindy's Note to Self:

I tell ya – I walked in PETRIFIED ~ but I walked out victorious!

But those who wait for the LORD's help find renewed strength; they rise up as if they had eagles' wings, they run without growing weary, they walk without getting tired.

(Isaiah 40:31)

A NOTE FROM ACTIV8HER

When the wait is long, weariness can quickly settle upon us. Cindy's note to self is a reminder that nothing other than God could offer her renewed strength. An important reminder for everyone. If you are weary, ask God for his strength that will renew yours.

NOTE TO SELF

Cindy's Note to Self:

I can do everything (all things) THROUGH HIM who strengthens me.

I am able to do all things through the one who strengthens me. (Philippians 4:13)

A NOTE FROM ACTIV8HER

There were several cards with this verse on them in Cindy's stash. One area she asked God for strength was with her desire for a husband. She prayed that God would send him at just the right time. She repeatedly asked for the strength to not give into any temptation that would cause her to miss out on God's best. What desire do you need strength to wait for?

NOTE TO SELF

Cindy's Note to Self:

God wants to use this circumstance for HIS GLORY.

But rejoice in the degree that you have shared in the sufferings of Christ, so that when his glory is revealed you may also rejoice and be glad.
(1 Peter 4:13)

A NOTE FROM ACTIV8HER

Whatever circumstance you find yourself in today, are you able to let God show off a bit and reveal his glory to others through it? Ask him for the strength to wait or hope, to relax and trust; to give or take. Begin to track how you see him answer.

NOTE TO SELF

Cindy's Note to Self:

Two WEAPONS of conquerors:
1. Fearlessness
2. Presence of God

And Moses said to him, "If your presence does not go with us, do not take us up from here." (Exodus 33:15)

A NOTE FROM ACTIV8HER

We have an arsenal of weapons at our disposal when it comes to conquering the attempts of Satan to throw us off track. We saw these two employed by Cindy many times: fearlessness and the presence of God. If God wasn't in it, she wasn't going there. Do you see an area of your life where you would like to acknowledge God's presence in a greater way?

NOTE TO SELF

Cindy's Note to Self:

You have a SECURE future with Christ.

What then shall we say about these things? If God is for us, who can be against us? (Romans 8:31)

A NOTE FROM ACTIV8HER

Every single day we experience opportunities to wonder if our future is secure. Cindy's note to self reminds us that in Christ we have what we need. Don't allow fear to trigger doubt that causes you to question if God cares. If you've had that thought, ask God to forgive you and reside secure in his care.

NOTE TO SELF

Cindy's Note to Self:

You can either worry yourself to death OR you can trust God to provide.

Indeed, he who did not spare his own Son, but gave him up for us all— how will he not also, along with him, freely give us all things?
(Romans 8:32)

A NOTE FROM ACTIV8HER

When our focus is on the natural it is only natural to worry. And worry offers nothing of value to your life. If you trust God to meet your needs, he is faithful to include some of your wants, too. ☺ Ask God to balance this out for you.

NOTE TO SELF

Cindy's Note to Self:

Go for the GREAT JOB and the GREAT HOME even if you have to do it afraid.

Do not be afraid, little flock, for your Father is well pleased to give you the kingdom.
(Luke 12:32)

A NOTE FROM ACTIV8HER

Are you limiting God's hand and your potential by holding back on setting high goals? Are you afraid to dream big dreams? Is it possible the desires he's placed in your heart are for his glory? Spend a few minutes asking God these questions. Then write down at least two big goals for yourself.

NOTE TO SELF

Cindy's note

God has an awesome plan for your life and you have not done enough wrong to screw it up.

GRATITUDE

Cindy's Note to Self:

God has an AWESOME plan for your life, and you have NOT DONE enough wrong to screw it up.

In him we have redemption through his blood, the forgiveness of our offenses, according to the riches of his grace.

(Ephesians 1:7)

A NOTE FROM ACTIV8HER

Your sins are covered by the blood of Jesus Christ. You can be forgiven for all the sins of your past by acknowledging that Jesus died for this purpose and by asking God to forgive you. Whether you have done this in the past or if this is the first time, write out a prayer acknowledging Jesus Christ as your Savior and asking him to forgive you of all the sins of your past. Commit to walking forward, acknowledging the riches of this grace.

NOTE TO SELF

Cindy's Note to Self:

Enjoy your life EVEN WHILE you have problems.

Blessed is the God and Father of our Lord Jesus Christ, the Father of mercies and God of all comfort, who comforts us in all our troubles so that we may be able to comfort those experiencing any trouble with the comfort with which we ourselves are comforted by God.

(2 Corinthians 1:3–4)

A NOTE FROM ACTIV8HER

It took some nudging, but eventually Cindy discovered that it was okay to pause from her problems and find joy in her life. One of her joys was helping other single moms who were experiencing a rough patch of their own. She was a comfort to them because Jesus was a comfort to her. What problem needs a pause and who needs your comfort today?

NOTE TO SELF

Cindy's Note to Self:

Praise be to the Lord, to God our Savior, who DAILY HEARS our burdens.

The Lord pays attention to the godly and hears their cry for help.
(Psalm 34:15)

A Note from Activ8Her

Day after day, our God is available to carry all that concerns us. What is heavy on your mind today that you can hand over to him to take for you? Thank him for his faithfulness to you day after day.

DATE: _____ / _____ / _____   S M T W TH F S

NOTE TO SELF

Cindy's Note to Self:

Uzziah's pride was rooted in his lack of THANKFULNESS. How's YOUR thankfulness?

But once he became powerful, his pride destroyed him. He disobeyed the LORD his God. He entered the LORD's temple to offer incense on the incense altar.

(2 Chronicles 26:16)

A NOTE FROM ACTIV8HER

Uzziah is an example of how we can begin well with our faith, but forget we serve God, not the other way around. Cindy must have been hit with the revelation that pride infects our ability to be thankful for God's influence and provision. Read the story of Uzziah and make a note to self: do not do this!

NOTE TO SELF

Cindy's Note to Self:

Help me today to see what is TRUE and NOBLE about YOU, others and myself.

Jesus said to him, "'You shall love the LORD your God with all your heart, with all your soul, and with all your mind.' This is the first and great commandment. And the second is like it: 'You shall love your neighbor as yourself.'"
(Matthew 22:37–39 NKJV)

A NOTE FROM ACTIV8HER

We love well when we can see the best in others and overlook their faults. Hopefully, it is easy for you to see what is true and noble about God. What about seeing the good in others? How about seeing the good in yourself? Explore this with the Holy Spirit today.

NOTE TO SELF

Cindy's Note to Self:

Happiness is:
staying GRATEFUL.

The LORD strengthens and protects me; I trust in him with all my heart. I am rescued and my heart is full of joy; I will sing to him in gratitude.

(Psalm 28:7)

A NOTE FROM ACTIV8HER

Short and sweet was Cindy's style. If you desire happiness–stay grateful. How has the Lord strengthened you? Protected you? How has he rescued you? Express your joy and gratitude to him.

NOTE TO SELF

Cindy's Note to Self:

I am THANKFUL.

Let the peace of Christ be in control in your heart (for you were in fact called as one body to this peace) and be thankful. (Colossians 3:15)

A NOTE FROM ACTIV8HER

"The absence of thankfulness is self-trust."* This note to self, reminds me of how committed Cindy was to search until she found the place in her circumstance where gratitude could be found. "Yeah, this is bad, but I am so thankful for…." Write your own note to self today as a reminder that there is always something to be thankful for.

–Kolleen

---

* Bill Johnson, "An Unlikely Weapon: Discovering the Power of Thanksgiving" (sermon).

NOTE TO SELF

Cindy's note

Christ left His PEACE for us because He knew we would NEED it 🙂

PEACE

Cindy's Note to Self:

Christ left HIS PEACE for us because he KNEW we would need it.

Peace I leave with you; my peace I give to you; I do not give it to you as the world does. Do not let your hearts be distressed or lacking in courage.

(John 14:27)

A NOTE FROM ACTIV8HER

He sure did! If we look at everything that is happening around us without allowing God to put his peace within us, we will be full of anxiety and fret. This is the day for a great exchange: Jesus' peace for your unrest.

NOTE TO SELF

Cindy's Note to Self:

Get in God's will and get the PEACE you're looking for.

In everything give thanks. For this is God's will for you in Christ Jesus.

(1 Thessalonians 5:18)

A NOTE FROM ACTIV8HER

Giving thanks in all things is the will of God and will bring you the peace you crave. What can you give thanks for today?

NOTE TO SELF

Cindy's Note to Self:

Lord, remind me *daily* that I am your INSTRUMENT and make me to know *without a doubt* that in you I am COMPLETE.

Therefore, since we have been declared righteous by faith, we have peace with God through our Lord Jesus Christ, through whom we have also obtained access into this grace in which we stand, and we rejoice in the hope of God's glory.

(Romans 5:1-2)

A NOTE FROM ACTIV8HER

As a single mother, Cindy set her focus on (1) Jesus and (2) her children. She did not want a divided heart, and although she desired a husband– she waited. She prayed for the day when God would provide her a man that would love her as Christ loves his own bride. But it would have to wait until her children were out of the house. She was strong in her decision that God would be her husband until the time was right. Whether married or single God is the only One able to complete you.

NOTE TO SELF

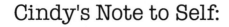

Cindy's Note to Self:

Lord, help me to enjoy this job of peace. Please fill my HEART and MIND with your thoughts, words and perspective of me. Reveal yourself to me in each moment and cause me to HUNGER and THIRST AFTER YOU in a new way. Remind me that I am your beloved.

I rely on the LORD. I rely on him with my whole being; I wait for his assuring word.

(Psalm 130:5)

A NOTE FROM ACTIV8HER

The thought of "relying on God with your whole being" should bring a wave of peace over your soul. Write out Cindy's prayer as it pertains to an issue in your life where you need to hear an assuring word.

NOTE TO SELF

Cindy's Note to Self:

I will pour out MY SPIRIT on your offspring, and MY BLESSINGS on your descendants.

For I will pour water on the parched ground and cause streams to flow on the dry land. I will pour my Spirit on your offspring and my blessing on your children.

(Isaiah 44:3)

A NOTE FROM ACTIV8HER

This is a promise of God that Cindy stood on and you can too. Rewrite this promise inserting the names of your children and any generation after that. Decide today that no matter what it looks like at this moment, you are going to stand on God's promise.

NOTE TO SELF

Cindy's Note to Self:

On some occasions God may purposely alter the evidences of HIS PRESENCE in order to bring the most benefit from our experience. Sometimes we receive the most benefit from seeing many visible "prints" of HIS INVISIBLE HANDS during a difficult season. Other times, we profit most from seeing fewer evidences.

I have told you these things so that in me you may have peace. In the world you have trouble and suffering, but take courage—I have conquered the world.

(John 16:33)

A NOTE FROM ACTIV8HER

God knows what we need even before we do. He knows what will produce a relationship with him that is set on a solid rock. When you feel God is distant, press into him. The Israelites experienced a wilderness. Jesus spent time in the wilderness. We will spend some time there, too. Look for the evidence, whether many or few—he hasn't left you.

NOTE TO SELF

Cindy's Note to Self:

How we gonna pay the bills....?
You have TWO CHOICES: you
can worry and worry and drive
yourself nuts OR you can trust me...

Then Jesus said to his
disciples, "Therefore
I tell you, do not
worry about your life,
what you will eat,
or about your body,
what you will wear."
(Luke 12:22)

A NOTE FROM ACTIV8HER

We can torment ourselves with worry when it comes to paying the bills or a myriad of other things. When we cling to God's Word and trust him, we walk in peace. What worry or worries can you trade for peace?

NOTE TO SELF

Connect with Activ8Her

Chrissy and Kolleen have been friends for over twenty years serving God, studying his Word together, and speaking life into each other.

In 2018 the Lord recreated a gifted ministry model to them and Activ8Her was born. The mission of Activ8Her is to activate and empower women to connect in relationships, build confidence in leadership, and develop courageous faith. The Activ8Her vision is to empower women to recognize their identity in Christ as key to living out their purpose.

At the realization that many single moms go without gifts on Christmas morning, in 2022 the ministry of Activ8Her held their first Christmas event, A Very Merry Cindy Christmas, in honor of our friend Cindy. All proceeds from the sale of this journal go directly to Cindy's Change. This is our commitment to continue to help change the world for Christ on behalf of Cindy.

To learn more about the ministry visit Activ8Her.org or connect with us at: activ8hernow@gmail.com or on one of our social media sites.

Made in the USA
Middletown, DE
19 October 2023

41113122R00121